OCCULT BLOOD

OCCULT BLOOD

Selected Poems

Paul Schwartz

&
AMPERSAND

Library of Congress Cataloging-in-Publication Data is available.

ISBN 978-0-9855681-0-8

Printed in the United States of America

10 9 8 7 6 5 4 3 2 1

For

SUSAN,

the tenth

AFTER THE BLITZ

Smoke clears
From this bombed-out life.
Perched high above the plain,
We take the census:
What's left?

I see dead people, says the kid.
Well, says I,
That's no big deal.
I've got them on my back
All the time.
Much more important:
What's alive?

That's where it gets interesting,
Says my ancient pal
(And he should know)

Growth from this point on is
Cancer.
But see that moving blip below?
Go check it out.
You just might be surprised.
And as for me,
I leave for Paris on the twelfth.

ARCANA

Can you tell the difference between Lino and
    Mono?
Where can you transfer from the IRT to the BMT?
Who was Otto Schmidlap?

There are riots in Egypt
The Sudan just split in two
What's happening in Burma?
Or is it Myanmar?

The things that matter
Have been winnowed

The fines are silly
But my own

I no longer care who wins

All that matters is
That pink in the morning sky

ARCHIVES

Thanksgiving in three days.
I've bought the bird,
Read the receipts.
All seems to be in place.

So,
In holiday-ish mood,
I take a break from work,
And think ahead,
As I do every year,
To that big day—
December seventh.
Pearl Harbor Day,
But not the one in Forty-one—
The one in Forty-four,
The day my phantom soldier daddy,
Max,
Succumbed to wounds in chest and legs,
Near Baccanello,
Emilia-Romagna,
Italia.

And
Thanks to
Archives of the New York Times,
I can construct
A picture of that day.

I read that, 'mongst other things,
The Reverend Harry Gladstone Greensmith died,
A bus killed two in Harvard Square,
Children will get more underwear,
Mrs. V. M. Bihn was charged with taking ration
    stamps,
Crazed Jersey man kills four, wounds two,
New York City's kosher poultry dealers strike,

The Blairstown Inn was sold,
The war's claimed 552,018 American lives to date,
And spinach is up but carrots down.

Then I see
8th Army Takes Lamone,
With some stuff 'bout Max's group,
But not 'bout Max, of course,
Or any other men who died that day.

Which tiny shards of fact,
Dear Max,
Bring me
As close as I will ever be to you.

BACON

I learned to cook bacon
From a Brit girl
Many years ago

First, melt butter in the pan
So it won't grip the strips
Like a bad mother

Don't let the bacon burn—
"Crisp is silly"

Cook eggs in the grease
Spoon fat over yolks
To just set them

I can still see her in my kitchenette
After forty years
Her round arms moving
And the look of concentration on her face
Though her name is gone

No stern mistress of the big pink map
But breakfast's queen

BELL CURVE

Life's a tale
of x and y
ordinate, abscissa
min and max
quadrants, octants
highs and lows

A bell-curve plot,
not smoothed,
each up and down a tale
of triumph or defeat

I'm at
x equals sixty-seven

The end of the line,
My story's end,
is someplace to the right

BIRTHDAY POEM

So, it's my birthday
And we've just had a good Chinese dinner
With clams and oysters
Live shrimp
And a bottle of champs.
Three old Brooklyn guys who go way, way back.

Now we're sitting 'round my living room,
And I'm the only one still drinking,
Because one of them has to drive the other home,
And the other can't handle the stuff anymore.

I go to the can
And when I come out,
The two of them are dozing,
Heads in the air,
Mouths wide open.

And it occurs to me:
This looks just like the dayroom
Of the Jewish Home for the Aged

I feel really good by comparison,
Sneak over,
And tickle the stockinged feet of a dozer,
Who wakes with a start.

And I laugh a good laugh
And think:
What a good, good day
This has been!

BLAKE

If you must rhyme for
eye,
why not break free,
use
sym-e-try?

So thought one
who walked 'round nude,
had visions
of great and awe-full
beauty,
and melded
printed page and canvas
on copper plate,
unpixilated

If only you could
heat your
cold, dead brain
in his magic furnace
burning bright

BOX CANYON

I've been coming down this trail for fifty years
And still don't know where I am,
Said the geezer in the Jeep.

I know what he means,
Though it's my first time here.

Where have I been?
Where am I now?
I have no idea.

Like the footprints on the sandy trail,
It's all a blur.

The canyon walls are lichen green.
It's cool.
And still.

I don't really care to know
What lies around the bend.

BRIGHTON BEACH MADELEINES

Old expat Pavel
(Not his real name,
He just feels that way)
Far from Brooklyn
Beachside boardwalk
Knish stands delis
Places where
"Eat that, it'll kill ya"
Used to be
Now all gone
Still tastes the
Salty, fatty, smokey
Things he chomped
Whilst walking from the El
Missing their yummy badness
Proudly made by real
Expats, old then
Now long, long dead
In barrels on the sidewalks
Overflowing baskets
Bagels, bialys
Onion-laced
The way they had them
"Over there"
Before that, too,
Was no more

BRINGS YOU BACK

What brings you back?

Little shell-shaped cookie
For that Frenchman.
Some old song?
Wet sand between your toes?

Me:

Morning glories

On a tall, tall fence.

Way back then.
So dense and purple,
You could barely glimpse
The private side,
Where rich kids lived.

Furtive urchins—
Squeezed through the gap,
Loudly used the seesaws and the swings,
Cool early seaside Sunday morn,
Then scampered back.

And now:

The scent
Of your perfume

Joy
Joy
Joy

BUMMED

At every
Entrance, exit, stop light, sign
A ragged man, woman, couple
With
Backpack, plastic bag, shopping cart, and
Sometimes,
Dog
Holds this handlettered sign:

HOMELESS
HUNGRY
COULD USE A BREAK TODAY
THANK YOU
(SMILEY FACE)

Slow down,
Speed up,
Look away,
Roll the window up

But know,
It's futile to resist

Shame comes
Guilt comes

You're done for the day
Sans bill in hand

BUNCHA BOYCHIKS TALKING

Buncha boychiks talking
Laughing

Diaspora voices roaring
As in vacant lots of old

But not the norm for many years

For opp-coastal need to fit
The Brooklyn brogue is quashed,
Replaced with who knows what

You want to fit
Can't sound brash and crude
They wouldn't understand

Flash back fifty years:
Speech test, NYU

Read the card that says
L-O-N-G   I-S-L-A-N-D
And report for
De-lousing of the vocal cords

To think we helped
Wipe out
That treasure

Feh!

BUTTER AND SUGAR

Do you remember,
Way, way back:

Farmer John's
Tumbledown stand,
Out on Route Seven,
Just north of town?

Racing home
With that great big bagful
of

Butter and sugar corn

They said you had to
Cook it
IMMEDIATELY
Or you'd lose that elusive taste:

Vermont on a summer's day

So race we did
And was it ever good!

(Don't salt the water)

CAME A MIGHTY WIND

Wind's picking up

Makes me uneasy,
Like a horse before the storm

Strange . . .

Rain's OK
Snow's OK

But this . . .

Cheek cracking
Drove Lear mad.
Tornado
Sent Dot to Oz

Cold's seeping
Through house's every crack

Shiver . . .

Get the magic candles ready

Could be the Pentecost

CANYONS

This street's a canyon
Poor walls
Steep and straight
No life in them
Just window rows
Up, down, across
Some shades are down
Some curtains shut
Can't see the sky from here
That's it
That's all

Think of
Box canyon,
Florence, Arizona.
As many walk it in a year
As walk this one each hour.
Wild sand orange walls
Streaked black and green
And when you round
Each secret bend
There is the sky
That's all
That's it

CARPE THAT DIEM

Bristlecone pine
Adds rings so slowly,
They can't be seen with naked eye.
So it may live forever.
Lichens, too.

But Highway One
Is here today
And gone tomorrow,
Or there yesterday,
And gone today.
The constant wind
And pounding waves
Will see to that,
To say nothing
Of what's hap'ning
Underground.

And so with us.

Fight it though we may,
Our bodies soon will seize,
Our brains will cloud,
Some cells will cease division,
While others will go wild.

No tommorows
Stretch out endlessly.

Carpe that diem while you may,
This may be
The final time
You see the light of day.

CATALPA

Another spring
And I'm still here.

I thought I'd be
That annual
You plant in spring.

I'd bloom all summer,
Die.
That's all.

But no,
I'm here,
Like that catalpa
You want cut down
In winter.

So ugly, hairy, gray.
Strange things hang
From every branch.

Why keep the thing?

And then,
It's spring!

Leaves so greeny.
Blossoms creamy.
Abundant.
Unrepentant.

Good thing
The chainsaw
Wouldn't start.

CHAPNIK

Here's how I see your life and me

You're fiddling a fox-trot
Ship's orchestra
SS Normandie
1939

Over the radio
News of Poland
Your home no more

So, dock in New York
Stay

Later,
The news, reality

Warsaw's gone
Your home
All gone

So, new home
You marry
Get a job at
The macaroni plant
Play in Polish restaurants some nights
(A great compliment, you say)
Have a son, twice your size
He's not into violin
Wants to play the vibes
But hey, it's an instrument at least
And he plays "Autumn Leaves"

And me, on Saturdays
With that love for the fiddle you found for me
The feel, the smell

Love for that old sheet music
With the Warsaw imprint
The music, love
And love for you, too
Gentle man
Sad but smiling always
No regrets

The Normandie is gone
The Ghetto's gone
That big old house in Rockaway is gone too,
    probably

You are gone,
Of course

But
I think of you
Every time I pick that fiddle up

The father I wished I had

CHOCOLATES

Momma kept her chocolates
Hidden in the linen closet

I found them there one day
While looking for a towel

And this did not seem odd to me
As I was my mother's son

I hid my pleasures,
Lest folks
Deem me

UNWORTHY

Of them

Which,
I knew,
I was

She taught me well

COELACANTH

Unnerving
To turn a jungle corner,
See a dinosaur

Or fishing,
Land a coelacanth

A fossil,
Millions years extinct

Fossils should stay fossil
Secrets should stay secret

That's where the horror lies

At the end of that line,
Now undead,
Is something
You don't want seen

Yeats' rough beast,
Flopping around
In the bottom of your boat
Ugly as sin

CORRIDO

Driving to Mexico
Doing a lot of that lately—
Damned teeth
Twenty years of neglect
Bites back
Ha!

But the vistas in the border lands
Gila Bend to Yuma
Make it all worthwhile

And the radio plays ranchera:
Tuba
Tuba
Tuba mirum
Tuba mirabilis

I don't know the words
Which is probably just as well
But sing along—
Vocalise—
As loud as I can

Mi corazon
Mi corazon
Corazon

CRAZY MAN

I've become that crazy man we used to see
Who walked round and round
and up and down

Once,
When you didn't see him weeks
You thought him dead

But he came back

Up and down
Round and round

I know, now
What happened to him

CRUMBLING

I'm with Joe and Sam.
Joe's eighty-five
And has,
I guess,
A month left
On his clock.
He's drooling,
Knows not where he is.
Takes half an hour
To get his diapered
Butt into the chair.
His body and his mind
Have downed the curve
In perfect sync.

Sam,
Who's minus ten,
Says,
You wouldn't know it,
Looking at him,
How many
Peaks we climbed.

I get it, Sammy.

Just took a header down the stairs.
A first
But,
I know,
Not the last.

CYCLE PLAIN TO SEE

The vulture and I
Share a moment in the sun

He's on his fencepost
I'm on my bench,
Not fifty yards away

We contemplate the bay,
That source of all things good—
Of death for him
Of life for me

And all around
The smell of salt,
Benign decay,
The cycle plain to see

Were I to die,
He'd pluck my eye
Tug at my flesh

And I'd not begrudge him that

I'd serve my purpose
In the scheme of things:

To nurture the living
In life and death

DEAR LILLIE

Why do I visit you?
Dear Lillie
You don't know me,
Though we meet each Wednesday
To chat and look at sky

I don't know you either
I know a woman in a chair
Who speaks in riddles
Softly, carefully,
Sounds each word fully
With pursed lips

What were you like
When you had your mind?

I can only guess

Grew up in Albany
Raised two proud
Black daughters
Now proud of you
Owned a dry-clean shop
You and your man
And a 16 acre spread
Where he grew vegetables
You cooked for dinner

This I have learned about you
But I can never know
The real you
And you can never know me
Can never know
Anything new

So why do I visit you?

27

I've asked myself this many times

The answer is
I'm paying my respects to
Dear Lillie
Who once was
And is no more

DEATH COMES SNEAKING IN

You expect to find him
Out on the highway,
Behind the bushes
In the dark

But in your living room?
Sneaking in

Yeah,
He's an old man
With hair in his ears

Sneaks in
When you're not looking
And takes what's yours

DEATHDREAMING

When the weather's bad,
I daydream death.
It's been cloudy lately,
So I've been doing this
A lot.

In these dreams,
I'm terminal
And think of what to do.

Today,
I planned a trip to Paris
Because I want to eat
Cheese and lardons
On a nice ficelle.

Asked you to come with me.
You laughed and said, "Of course,"
Then went to your computer.
(You're so good at this.)

"Where do we stay?" you asked.
Latin Quarter or Montparnasse.
Two weeks.
Say, twenty thousand bucks.

The future happens,
Plan for it or not.

Of course,
We think we're immortal.
How else could we fall asleep
And risk not waking up?

DEMENTIA

De:
Get rid of
Lose it

Mentia:
Mind
Something of the brain

Lose brain?

No

Still brain
An altered brain
Still mind

Some drug it
Whack it purposely

So,
Maybe good?

Sun's out
Sky's blue
My demented friend is happy
Remembers
So long ago
Walking home from school
Got her degree!

Sees kids outside
Thinks, what could they want?
What should she give them?

So kind
So nice

Big smile
No fear
No pain

Could be worse

DESCENT

What have I done?
Not much,
I think.

Except one thing—
the thing I thought I'd never do—
I have grown old.

And done that pretty well,
I think.

I think,
Not bad.
Strange, yes,
But not bad.

I'm not singing Whitman's song,
But this part of the curve's not bad.
And I can see tomorrow, too,
Which I often could not do,
In that rowboat on the open sea.

DOPPELGANGER

I look around—
I am not like you.
I'm odd.
You could not understand
What makes me tick.

I've dragged this stuff around
Lifelong—
A heavy sack of sad, sad junk.

But

That oddness that I revel in
Could be conceit.

Because

Today I met
My doppelganger,
And we share this:

Same age.

Same last name,
Which is not the one we had at birth.

Fathers we never met,
New York City Jews,
Killed in action, World War II,
Interred in European graves.

Mothers who remarried,
Craved normalcy,
Changed our names,
And never mentioned this
'Til we were grown.

One day, in middle age,
We set out to find those graves,
Embrace our oddness and our ghosts,
And weep,
And say,
"Hi pops. It's me,
Whoever that might be."

I could ask my doppel,
"Do you think you are unique?"

But he really needn't answer,
And I no longer have to ask.

DOWITCHER KNOWS

Here it is
All sun and blue.
Warm breeze,
Bay calm.
Avocets, gulls
Asleep, like stones.
But dowitchers
Frenetic, busy.
What do they know?

Walking bay shore, south,
I think: forever
This will be
Warm sun
And blue
Always.

But

Forecast says no.
Radar says rain.
How do they know?
Magic!
Like dowitcher.

Turn toward home
And there—
Far northwest, twenty miles—
Massive clouds
Announce tomorrow's rain.

I think:
Trust dowitcher.

'

DRUMBEAT, OUTSIDE MY WINDOW
LAST NIGHT

Rosie's looking in the pink this dawning,
but last night
I dreamt of death—
again.

Not mine,
but women I have known,
and from there to those who'll follow,
and then to me.

And falling down
(ashes, ashes),
sometimes getting up,
but sometimes not.

And how you want to leave
a certain way,
say, looking down
on your favorite mountain town,
above it,
so you can feel yourself leaving.
Going up,
not down.

But you won't go that way.
You'll just go.
And since you'll have no say in this,
it will have to do.

ENDGAME

This play's 'bout death,
Not chess,
So misnamed,
But catchy

Death's the poets' topic number one
(Love's number two),
But why?

May be because
It's one true unknown—
The dead don't grant interviews—
And you can only guess

So 'twould help to know
Something 'bout it
If you're after truth

And you can learn
By watching people die,
Which some will volunteer to do
Under guise of helping,
But you will be
The ultimate voyeur

And so
I wonder
As the play unfolds
What did he know?
And how did he know it?

EVERYONE DYING

They keep coming:
Bad phone calls
Sad e-mails

Makes me think:
What's the point of the morning rise
Take a shower
Pay the bills

The Seven Samurai

EXPAT SONG

Gray skies here
Freedom rings from every
But you can't get
A decent hot dog

My country 'tis
Not easy loving you
So leaving now
Not nor ever having been
A member of
But always second class
Or worse

East West
North South
And every angle in between
On foot in dead of night
In steerage
Hop a freight
Or fly first class

If your skin's too dark, too light
If you like your sex a certain way
Have the wrong beliefs, or none
Just go
Learn the language
And the coin
Get a job
Breathe free
Live free
But
Send your ashes
Home

What I would not give
For a decent knish

FINAL GIG

We gather 'round the dying
Hoping for insight

Living long, it's said,
Will make one wise
And the dying may oblige—
After all,
This is their final gig

No work tomorrow
Forget the litter box
And screw the bills

This is it

An audience!
The chance to cry:
Mehr Licht! Mehr Licht!
Get the respect you missed

They'll eat it up

So gather 'round
Lean in
Listen closely
Turn the recorder on

You might get
What you've been searching for

Or
You might just hear
A rattle

And

"I'd rather be
In Philadelphia"

FLASHBACKS

One thing leads to another,
Of course.
Like this:

Whilst taking out the trash,
I pass a purple-berried bush,
As I have many times before,
But this time wonder:
Huckleberry?

So, look it up and
Yes,
Huckleberry!

Then,
Flashback to Coney Island beach,
Many years ago.

My hero, The Good Humor Man
(How I longed to be
The Good Humor Man!)
Sold huckleberry Good Humor pops
(My favorites)
For just a few days each summer.

So I guess,
Back then,
They used real, fresh huckleberries
In their huckleberry ice cream pops.
Seasonal, you see.

How quaint!

Then,
Flash to the lovely Audrey
Singing "Moon River"

To her huckleberry friend
(Would he were me).

But,
Why "huckleberry" friend?

So, look it up.

And find that
Huckleberry,
Once, when that was possible,
Meant little, kind, and good.

So it all makes sense,
As it always does,
When past meets present
On your way to the trash.

FORECAST

Days, weeks go by.
There are people sleeping under bridges,
Scrounging the dumpster behind my home.
My friends will be foreclosed—
I send them money,
Give five bucks to a man with no shoes.
Lies are told.
Rights taken away.
The things we fought for, going, gone.
The world has gone to pot.

But it's quiet here.
Not a peep.
The news is all sports,
Pregnant starlets,
And the weather, of course.

Quiet.

What will it take to stir the beast?
More than we'll get, I'm sure.

It rained today,
But it's quiet,
And it'll stay that way . . .

Until?

FORTY BELOW

What I used to feel
Was death around the bend

You couldn't see around that bend
Headlights before dawn
Just picked out ruts in snow
That's what you focused on
Tried not to think about
That sheer drop-off to the right
Windows rolled up
Heater full blast against the cold
The only sound

Hoped no one was coming
From the east
That would do it
Sure

It was the cold
Death 'round that bend

Brave this to save an hour
'Round the mountain
Know that hour
Could be the last
Off that sheer drop
Down that ravine
Hidden for weeks
And frozen solid

So, think of summer
Vermont days
Back sixty years
Boys in CCC
Hacking out this mountain road
And singing

A hundred bottles of beer on the wall

Knuckles white
Down down that final grade
And out
At last

GREAT BIG TREES

Imagine
Getting out of stir—
Been twenty years—
Back to what was home

Sit quietly
And stare
At great big trees
Where saplings grew

Muscles, organs
Shrink,
As do expectations,
But green just grows
And grows
And grows

Doesn't need your daily gaze,
And that's both comfort
And a source of dread

Behold:
Your future,
Verdant grave

HAPPY BDAY, BUB

Today would have been your bday, Bub.
So, Happy happy bday!
I miss you so much.
We'd have gone to lunch
Or dinner at your fave.
I'd give you a big present.
(How many years did it take for me
to get that right?)
We'd talk of growing old.
And all that we had seen and done.
And what we might do next.

Will this ever end?
Maybe not.

The feeling's less intense
But still there.

HAPPY NEW YEAR AMERICA

Here's another one ending
A new one beginning
But not slouching
More like limping
Out of Alabama
Or another beet-red place

Sad sight indeed

You'd be a sap
To fear that mangy thing
Fat on fast food
Sclerotic
With bad teeth
Out of place
On this warming, changing orb

It's gonna watch that
Crystal ball go down
Down down
Resolve to lose a few
Win the lottery
Get that Kenyan outta there
And the gummint off its back

Grab that Chinese shotgun
Turn on Fox News and
Blow out what's left
Of its brains

HER MUSEUM

The walls of her museum are
Strangely bare.

A few bland things,
Chosen for their color.
Old hats on hatrack.
Mirrors.

A poverty of art.

But here I see some photos,
Gathered in a frame.
A large family group
(with dog),
Victorian dress.
Two stiff portraits
(Mom and Dad?).
A field and barn.
And a little pen-and-ink,
"First Snow,"
Dated 1897.

Midwest?

What richness!

HERE'S TO ALL THE WISE ONES

Across the deserts,
Through the parted seas,
Asleep naked 'neath the stars.
Here now,
But not sure how or why.
Thinking of those little bits—
Advice from wise ones
Now long gone.

I fretted once,
O'er crooked things
In and on walls—
Obsessed.
(Those who've built will know.)
'Til a wise old guide
Told me the truth:

A coat of plaster
Covers
A multitude of sins.

HOPE SPRINGS ETERNAL

Hachiya hangs from 'simmon tree.
Bright shocking orange
Mid leaves dark green

Pluck it,
But don't bite.
For,
If you can hold it
Tightly in your hand,
You won't get it
Past your lips

It's wonderful,
She said,
When dead, dead ripe
And oozing juice

To ripen,
Freeze it solid,
Then take it out
And let it sit
'Til it decays

So,
I thought,
Maybe,
Just maybe,
There's hope
For me

HOW IT'S DONE

Heron
Stands on one leg,
Then the other,
Sometimes both.
Motionless.
A long, long time.
Stares at water.
Waits for fish.
Strikes.
Swallows.
That's it.
Wonder if he thinks at all.
What he thinks of if he does.

I
Sit on my behind.
Stare at screen.
Motionless.
A long, long time.
Wait for thought.
Write it down.
Clitter clitter.
Clack clack.
That's it.
That's all.

HOW LONG?

Grief's from "heavy," "grave."
And grave's where it begins,
Or ashes, if you choose.

Mourning's from "memory."
Remember,
Pow!
Then grieve.

How long's grief's season?
A year?
Neat. Biblical.
Two, three, more?
How long's too long?

Docs who write the DSM,
Who decide what's sick and sane,
Say grieve too long and you're a
"Complicated Case."
Pills may be prescribed.

I say, don't judge.
We're all different.
Mope years more
If you must.
Or just make sure
Dead's really dead
And fly, fly off.
It's up to you.

(I did four years)

IF

If . . .

If I . . .

If you . . .

If we . . .

If only . . .

If—
Short, pregnant word—
Two letters!

Maybe,
A possibility

Like an unripe Hachiya.

IN MEMORIAM

Read the obits every day
But Sunday's best and biggest

Check to see who's gone

There's prose in columns,
Six point type:

Born 123
Did XYZ
Devoted this
Beloved that

But there,
Bottom right,
"In Memoriam,"
Is poetry:

Miss you like crazy,
In my heart forever,
Can't believe
It's been a year

IN THE HOUSE OF SHIELDS

Sitting in a bar
Old bar
Like the one
I grew up in:
My uncle's
Royal Bar and Grill
Sutter & Essex
East New York
Brooklyn

Remembering sawdust floor
Nice stale-beer smell
Long, long mirrored wall
A hundred bottles, doubled
Dark wood
Red stools
Brass rail

Guys came in after work
For a beer and a shot

Unk gave me nickles
To play skee ball
Shuffleboard
But not pinball
(Too tricky for a kid)

I didn't understand a word
Not then
Not now
But it felt warm and good

And still does
After two negronis

IN VERNAL FALL

This time,
Back east,
We'd burn dead leaves,
Peer through perfume smoke
At bare slopes,
Turn the garden under—
Black stalks to green
The promised spring—
Put away the tools
That kept
The summer's green at bay—
Frost would do that now—
And wait for snow

Only here,
In vernal Fall
On California hills,
More green blades
Poke through brown
With each cold rain—
New life

In the dying
Of the year

IN YOU

In you I had
a fifty-three MG TF
Amati
Strad

In countless graveyards there lie
Ramblers
Kazoos
Comb-and-paper rigs

So I feel no shame
Well, some

The man is drunk
or crazy

Let him rave
Poor thing

INTO WHAT?

Unlike you guys,
I'm not immortal.
I don't buy green bananas,
And each morning's a surprise.

So, save your breath.
You drop round me like flies.

I live each day
Like it's the last.
But, sad to say,
It's hard for me
To boogie.

And that's the rub.

I'm someplace strange.
I've missed my flight.
None for another day.

I walk outside.
The sun shines brightly.
Step off the curb

Into what?

JEWISH FOOTBALL

Uproar!
These guys are yelling at each other,
Pounding the table,
Hands wildly flying,
As they sip Courvoisier,
And puff their Montecristos,
High on the words,
The heady argument,
The sheer joy of
Cerebral coupling.

The Shiksa is alarmed!
Runs in to see who might be harmed.
She doesn't understand
Jewish football.

JOURNEY'S END?

Journey.
From Old French: A day.

Then, how far you'd
Walk in one:
Chartres to Rambouillet
Nevers to Decize.

Then less: Vermont,
The distance between towns,
Three miles—
You'd do it in an hour.

Or more—free will:
Sweet Betsy from Pike
Crossed the wide mountains
With her lover Ike.

Or forced: Bataan March
The Middle Passage
Last train from Madrid
Boxcar to Belsen.

And at the end
That B and B
Called Journey's End,
Where, old man,
Having walked
A mere four miles,
Felt in every fiber, joint,
Takes off boots,
Sips mulled wine,
Stares at fire,
And wonders if he's there.

JUST PLAIN UGLY

16th Street BART stop
Streets coated with slime
Oh yum for vermin
Both furred and feathered

And we are living in it!
Cutting our toenails
Picking our nits
Peeing in doorways
Looking for hits
And tricks

Were we born like this?
Or did we devolve?
And why?

I walk the street,
Depressed.

Then, preschool's out.
Children run around,
Chase each other,
Whooping, joyful,
Sweet, and pure

How long will it take
Before they become
The ones
I can't look at?

LAST JEW IN KABUL

There used to be
(Used to be)
A minion here
Merchants
Wives & kids
Alone here but
Together

A tribe
A minion
Alone, but not

Years went by
The others died
Or left
Were not replaced
(Taliban would only
Let you do so much)

He stayed

His shop was spare
One room
One hanging bulb
He lived upstairs

Wife died
They had no kids

He stayed

Every Friday
He shut the door
Turned off the light
Went upstairs to pray

He didn't know the prayers
He didn't know the words
He didn't even
Know his God

He stayed

He knew

He was

He stayed

LENNY'S LATEST

Better an old poet
Old singer
Dancer

They think:
He can still do it
She can still sing it
And isn't that just great!

They don't know:
It's easier
With each passing year

Reach a point,
You can do it in your sleep.
Sometimes,
That's all you do

The voice is barely there.
So much wisdom!
But, I know,
He's enjoying this joke

As the latest
Suzannes, Maryannes
Softly, sweetly
Echo his raspy croak

LEROY

Leroy was of a long-gone breed,
Of a long-gone place,
Of a long-gone time.

A little, dapper, gay black man,
Dressed in English suits
And wing-tip shoes,
With a clipped, made-up accent
And a little, clipped mustache.

Lived on the West Side,
West End Ave.,
New York, New York,
Among the refugees,
Back when they were still there,
Reading "Aufbau"
And listening to "The Muntzenmier Hour"
On EVD AM.

A sunny kind of guy,
Who never let on what he'd been through.
You always got a big smile and Hi! from him,
And you knew
(He didn't have to say it)
That if the day was good for him,
It would be good for you.

Ms. A. knew.
Four-eleven, blue-haired, tailored, and
    fur-trimmed,
She covered that number on her arm,
And smiled and smiled and smiled,
Especially when the sun shone
On West End trees.

Reminded her

Of Unter den Linden,
Long ago and far away.

Leroy held the door for her.
They chatted, giggled, smiled and smiled
As they rode the elevator
Down to West End Ave.
And ambled down Broadway.

What a pair!

Those old lives of pain
— Tacit —
No need to bring it up.
The sun is out on West End Ave.!
Another day is here for us to share!

Years went by.
One day she died.
Left everything to him,
So that, maybe, he could quit his job,
Learn German,
And read "Aufbau" to her ghost,
As they listened to the "Muntzenmier Hour."
Or hold the door and smile at Mrs. B. and Mr. C.
As they toddled out to sunny West End Ave.

Makes perfect sense to me.

LICHENS

mycobiont
+
phycobiont
=
symbiont

110°F
noon
South Maricopa Wilderness

Rocks too hot to touch
Even the lizards can't stand it

Yet, on the north-facing slopes
The lichens are alive

Parti-colored fools in hell

Surely, their genes will be needed
When it really heats up

LIGHTEN UP

Let's take a nature walk
And gripe:
Look what they've done to California!
All these plants and trees—
Ice plant, fennel, mustard, yooks—
Nonnative!
And the critters—
Foxes, possums—
Ditto!
To say nothing of us humans—
Not an Indian in sight!

Can you imagine
What it must have looked like
Before the White Man came?
(And here a tear is shed)

No, I can't

I'm from New York City
We have Central Park—
A plant museum—
And a nesting hawk
Is prime time news

At least you have the Bay
These hills
And don't forget the birds

Thanks to you
They will always be

So lighten up
And let's enjoy this sunny day

LISTENING TO BRAHMS IN FOG

Fog this morning.

Listening to Kogan play the Brahms.
Lovely, like the fogscape,
but warm, not cold.

Thank you, thank you, Leonid!

Then, remembering my recording of it,
how much it meant to me when young,
but lost the fiddler's name,
though I could see his picture on the sleeve.

Until—
Christian Ferrar!
(I thought.)

But search led to Ferras,
and a bio,
and a death—
by suicide—
Paris,
1982,
age 49.

And that depressed me.

So, still listening to Kogan—
(lovely, warm, and, now, bittersweet)
This one's for you,
Christian!

LISTENING TO K. 581 IN THE MORNING

If I could write this,
I would gladly die,
right here, right now.

But he was only 33!
Half my age.
How did he know?

Could he see death
in his room at dawn,
or pass him in the street,
or smell him,
brush against him?

Or in that time,
when 50 was old age,
did he just expect him,
accept him?

Or, in that cold garret,
sick, in debt,
welcome his offer of relief?

There, in that opening measure,
bittersweet,
lies his understanding,
his astounding understanding,
of his life
and ours.

LISTENING TO THE PATHETIQUE

Over half a century,
the meaning of a piece,
a poem,
a word
changes
with you.

At sixteen,
listening to this
in my darkened room,
it was my world
and I was in it,
drowning at its sad conclusion.

Now,
I see HIS despair,
not my own.

Ha!
I have outlived him!

LOVE POEMS

This is a great surprise . . .
All those love poems
Turn out to be true!

In a way

Especially e.e.
and Donald Hall:

Your heart in my heart,

Death no parens,

Scream and yell sometimes

But, mostly,
The wonder

That every day
Day after day
Year after year

You are still here

Impossible, it seems,
But true

MARKET STREET

Oakland Chinatown
Does it for me
Every time,
But any Chinatown
Will do.

Picking my way
Through crowds,
Food stacked
On noisy, dirty streets,
Walking sideways,
Bags raised above my head,
Laughing with the laughter.

Don't get the joke,
But it's funny anyway.

Then flashback sixty years,
Opp-coastal,
Pan-European,
Teeming,
Blake Ave.,
Brooklyn.

Shopping with my Gran.
Picking my way
Through pushcarts,
Barrels, boxes, crowds,
But nearer ground,
Since I'm a little kid.
I get the joke and laugh.

How I loved that scene!

And now
There flashes

On the inward eye
A little old babushka,
Dressed head to toe in black,
Biting a fish
To see if it's fresh

METAMORPH

Call me Gregor

I have morphed into
An old bone bag
Stooped
Inert
Four limbs still
But tommorow
Is another day

Used to strive
And scheme
To do
Acquire
Win
Live large

Now torpid
Everything is small
Except the sky
(Bigger)
And plants
(Gigantic)

Only they make sense

Today it was
Scotch broom

Like me,
An alien

MICROTOMING A LIFE

First tranche,
One to twenty:
Confusion and strife

Second tranche,
Twenty-one to sixty-five:
Struggle and victory

Put each thin slice
Under the lens
And peer
At scenes
Rich with life

A Leeuwenhoek
In wonder

At having survived
And triumphed

Third tranche,
Sixty-six to when?

Put eye to lens
With trepidation

What do you see?

Possibility
Mystery
And

Of course

The end

MIGHT BE SIBELIUS

Early morning's best for poetry,
When mind is still in dream's embrace
And body's soft complaint is quelled
By simple plunk in chair

Put that sweet gift to use:
Time saving's extra hour of darkness,
So sweet to those who love to see
First light in eastern sky
And pinky streaks evolve and spread
The color of another day

Might be the sense
That body's presage of despair,
That dumb alarm
Bawling its dire dawn warning,
Might be ignored,
Or,
It might just be Sibelius

MOONDOG

Heard another poem 'bout Moondog.
I was privileged to have seen him
Long ago
In all his horny Vikingness

I was leery
But David,
Who was so much nervier than I,
Went up to him and said,
Hi, my name is David.
Had a coversation with the man,
Learned he wrote music,
And became a friend

Years later,
After he had left his post on 6th and 53rd,
I learned his story,
Complete as it could be

Now, I think of him
Every now and then,
And realize why
He frightened me:

I could have been him
And all that implied

Bad then

Good now

MORNING, AS USUAL

This day is as gray
As what's left of my hair.

Woke to chest pains.
Lay there and waited to die,
But, as I did not,
Rose and looked outside—

At the sky,
For the absent sun,
At the parking-lot blacktop,
For that slick
That is witness to rain.

Then staggered to coffee,
Turned on machine,
Staggered to screen,
To write down
The poem
That may have been the heat
That radiated
In my chest
But did not kill me,
Just woke me up.

Little things of the day or the dream
Are the only things I understand,
The only things that make sense,
The only things I can write down
Without feeling like a fool.

MUSTARD

Mother of all cabbages—
Cauliflower, broccoli, kale,
And those cute sprouts from Brussels—
We salute you,
Your Yellowness,
Queen Mustard!

Brassica juncea,
Of family Crucifera
(For petals four, in a cross)
Six stamens—
Four tall, two short—
Spread waisthigh lemony yellow lovely
In every fallow field in Spring

As yummy to the taste as to the eye,
Stir-fried or in a soup,
Pickled, too, the Asian way.
What would the gherkin do without your seed?
How could the hot dog
Reach its gastronomic height
Without your stripe or squiggle
Down the middle?

No shrinking violet, you.
Strong, Boudicca-like,
Your jaunty golden empire spreads from sea to sea,
And none dare call you weed.

MY BODY

This thing
that carries me about
is getting old.

It used to thrill me,
now I wait for it to fail,
list'ning to it creak,
wary of the leak,
and fretting at the pain du jour.

I no longer know it.
And when I see it in the mirror
(I used to like to do that — sad!),
I am just shocked.

Still, it's all I've got.

So we totter about,
tripping the light dysmorphic.

MY TREE IN WINTER

My tree is bare,
Branches gnarled

Each day
I search

Look for buds
Look for a sign
Of green
Of Spring

So far,
Not a thing

Like groundhog,
I crave Spring
And green

But squirrel
Finds baldy useful:
A shortcut to the roof

So I'll look at tree
A different way:

Useful
And, yes,
Quite beautiful

NIGHT-BLOOMING CEREUS

When you throw your lot in
with luna moths
you're apt to keep strange hours

3 am
23rd Street PATH station
I watch rats at play
doze
listen for the Ho-boke train

The trick to working nights is to
get to sleep before the sun comes up

If you can't do that,
then gin's the thing

These guys are strange
but I feel right at home

At the margin

Waiting for the night to end

NINE SLASH ELEVEN

My one is gone

Oh,
Maybe
I will be
Some more

But
My one
Is
No more

And
I can't
Describe
My pain
In words

So when they say,
You MUST do this
You MUST feel that
To honor those
Who lost their lives
On THAT day,
I admit,
With shame,
That, try as I may,
I can't really care enough
For anyone else's ones
As I watch,
Again and again and again,
My one
Sail through smoky air
Toward nothingness

NO ADVICE FOR THE AGED

I'm very old
But most unwise.

(Yo, Polonius!
Just shut it!)

Read Skinner once,
On aging.

He's eighty,
Playing chess with some kid,
And thinks:
The brain's an organ,
Just like your rectum.
Why should it be immune to age?

And, of course,
He knows it's not.

Still, . . .

He can beat that kid,
Because he has
What the kid has not:
Experience.

But you're no kid.
And when I'm near you,
Gaga,
I'm thirteen again.
A complete and total mess.

At least the acne's gone.

NO PLACE TO GO

Watched biopic 'bout this famous man
(Wrote songs)
Made by another famous man.

Many tears were shed,
Much wistfulness,
As lovers spoke of him.

And then
I realized—
He could be anyone,
Even some furry thing,
And it would be the same:

Your love
No longer
Has
A place
To go.

That was yesterday,
And now
I weep.

NO STING-A-LING

I walked through vacant lots
On the way to school.
Tried not to step on
Carcasses of dogs
Hidden in the grass.

There were dead rats in the yard,
Flattened pigeons,
Dead cats in the street.
And on the beach at Coney once,
Dead chickens at high tide,
Among the gobs of tar.

Death was everywhere
When I was twelve.
At the movies,
On TV,
In the books I read,
And in my dreams.

He frightened me.

Grandma, Grandpa, Mrs. Klein,
Out in the street on a gurney
In the rain.

Death got to Dad before I could,
Held Mom in his embrace,
Sucked all the joy from home.

He lived in the closet in the hall.
No one but me noticed.

And then, one day
I could see a life without him.
Turned my back on him,

Flipped him the bird,
And left him in the dust,
Where he remains today.
Necessary but pathetic.

Yes,
I had help
(I was twelve and I'm not that strong):
Mad Magazine.
Twenty-five cents a copy
(Cheap!)

NOVEMBER SONG

Listening to music
By some genius
Who died at thirty-one,
Singing the song
Of a wise old man

And reading Dylan
(The real one;
Not that whiner)
Who died at forty,
Yet wrote
So many words
That sang
His lovely voice

If I lived twice as long
And wrote and painted
Day and night,
My oeuvre
Would not be worth
One tenth
Of one percent of theirs

Which makes me sad

But

The sun shone today.
Did some work,
Slapped on some cobalt blue,
And put these pixels on the screen

And that will have to do

OBIT

My old boss is dead at 83.

There's his picture in the *Times,*
looking like he did 40 years ago,
when I stood in an elevator with him
as he spoke of being up all night, writing.

I saw something of myself in him then—
It wasn't the fortune he was after.

He saw something of himself in me, too—
that boychik thing.

Sensing that, I played him shamelessly,
and had the best year of my life.

Now he's gone.

And I'm taking the next car.

OCOTILLO

Bony fingers,
gnarled

Nails painted orange

Outstretched
against the sky

Ocotillo!

OLIVES

The news these days is almost always bad.
Makes me wonder
How my mother felt as she
Read the papers back in '44
While my father fought his way
Up the boot.

It's REALLY bad from Middle East,
Where the crazies on both sides
Destroy each other every day.

Which brings me to olives.

One thing the "Settlers" seem to like to do
Is burn the Arabs' olive trees.
This loss is tragic, because
It's many years ere these trees bear fruit,
And they can live for thousands more.

They'll be there long, long
After all these nuts have gone
To their well-earned hells.

Olives seem to like the coasts,
So California suits them fine.

On my street,
Built more than thirty years ago,
There is a very tall,
Very old
Olive tree.

I guess it was there when they built the street,
So they decided to leave it where it was.

It's LOADED with black olives.

I gathered some and put them in a brine.
Tasted them day by day.
After a week they were sublime!

Oh, big old olive tree,
So full of life,
If someone burned you down for spite
My heart would break.

ON FALLING APART, OR NOT

What does it mean
When the books on your shelves
Aren't alphabetized
By author
Or by title,
Just moved from the table,
And thrown into
Some empty space?

You'll have to dust eventually.
And the yard!
Weeds and pots and mayhem.

Will you be that story in the news,
Where the cops go to that house
Because the neighbors called
About the smell
And they have to dig a path
Through piled-up junk
To find you in the bathtub?

Hey, look!
The sun's out!

Lemme outta here!

ONCE UPON A TIME

Once upon a time
I met a girl who boiled with life
Teetering about
On three-inch espadrilles
Black hot pants
White peasant blouse

I thought,
What would it be like to live like that?
Happy in a sad, sad world

I found out

And forty years later
I found, again
The back side of the colored page

Ripped by the wind
and blown away

Turning, turning
It fell to ground

Blank

White

ONE-LEGGED COYOTE

Demented
Lila's lost her mind
They say

Gibbers
Makes no sense
They say

Can't read the Rorschach blot

But
Like Finnegan
Or Pound
Puts words together
Well
I'd say

I'd say
One-legged coyote
Gets it done
But Lila's words
Are poems
More than
Those Cantos

PALESTRINA

Now here comes Palestrina
On the radio at night.

My neighbor's home.
Turns on that awful stuff
That shakes the walls and
Sets the glasses tinkling.

Over and over,
That stupid, vapid bass.

I up the volume in defense.

Swirling, welling,
Swooping up and down,
Four hundred something years,
He drowns that crap flat out.

I don't know Latin.
I don't know God.
But I am glad to say
I know
PALESTRINA.

PAPER

Seven years
Says CPA
Is what the IRS requires.
But I had room for
Seventeen, at least,
So paper, paper,
All that paper,
Boxes marked
Paid this
Paid that
Business
Personal
And good old "Misc,"
Is what my garage shelves contained

And then I sold the house—
No more garage—
And shredded
For what seemed a week,
And still,
So many boxes left!

So,
Throwing caution to the winds,
I put them in recycle bin
And felt the pain
And wept
For life
Diminished and transformed

PIN

Blind Milton,
exactly my age when he died,
considered how his light was spent.

Not well, I gather.

Me, I see the screen just fine
but consider:
What if I could not turn it on?

What if one day
that thing that must contain
four to eight letters and/or digits,
no spaces, dots, or commas
— CASE SENSITIVE —
fell from its synaptic perch in cranial ganglion,
hit the floor,
shattered,
scattered,
and could not be found?

Then,
helpless,
screen dark,
cursor locked,
would I consider how my PIN was spent?

POSTWAR BOWLING

I love my little bowling place,
With its
Fifty-year-old frieze
Of neon rocket ships and stars.

Sunday AM,
The geezers' favorite time:
No kids, quiet,
And a buck and a half a game 'til noon.

I'm not bowling well today,
But to my left,
Grayed Remy breaks one-eighty,
And to my right,
Bald Otto's score is out of sight.

Remy's from Viet Nam.
Little guy.
Fought on the losing side,
As did I.

Otto's eighty-one.
From Dusseldorf,
His accent is still thick.
Maybe his dad killed mine
In the snowy Apennines.

Time,
Ten pins,
Shiny lanes,
And California magic
Heal all wounds.

Strike!

RE: PAST

How lovely is the past!
Blue sky,
Warm breeze,
And gentlest surf.
Back to belly
In the softest, warmest bed.
Hand on breast
And tongue in ear.
Sweetest scent
And softest breath,
Drifting off to deepest sleep.

You can skip the raucous tracks,
Play the best ones over
And over
And over.
You are so young,
And healthy,
And alive.
There's plenty in the fridge and bank.
You laugh!
No pain in mind or joint.
No end to bliss.

Too good to let go of.

But

Present's here.
The mind's less sharp.
The body aches.
You are alone.

Look around:
The walls need paint.
That armchair's looking old.
Clothes are going out of style.
New drivers license pic's of someone else.

Rain today.
Stiff wind.
Annoying clock is all you hear.
Tick
Tick
Tock

REALITY

True story:

On his deathbed,
Father tells his writer son
He's not, as thought,
A proper British gent
(Public school voice
And clipped mustache)
But Polish Jew,
Survivor of the Holocaust

First,
SCHOCK!
Then,
LIBERATION!

The writer knows—
If dad is not
What he appears to be,
The same applies to him

And,
Since tink'ring with reality
Is what a writer does,
Absence of one etched in stone
Means he can write a fuzzy one

But don't you need a real,
Else you drift off,
Who knows where,
And bang up on some shore,
Confused and dazed?

Well,
You could make one up

RECALL

I believe
That every thing
We've ever seen,
Heard, felt, or smelt
Is safely stored
Up there
Enskulled
And will be there
'Til we cease to be

We call this memory
When brain-screened

On purpose or
By accident

It can be sweet,
Downright ugly,
Or both at once.

Viz:

This morning,
Coffee cup in hand,
I sit at screen and think:
That song . . .
What was it called?
Da da, da da, da da, da da!
From forty years ago

So pull down vid and see
A long-dead golden girl,
Bouffant, mini,
Pulsing rock beat

And then

Tears
Tears
For every love and friend
Now gone

Da da, da da, da da, da da

REQUEST

Woman called this in,
Late-night radio:

Mahler was the fave
Of my husband,
Al.

Especially the Fifth.

Could you play the
Adagietto
For me
For him?

I once read:

Why, in music,
Do we crave
This pain?
These tears?
This living
Death?

Does it
Dull the longing
Or make it worse?

Whatever,
Play it for me.

Make it a double.

ROYAL BAR AND GRILL

They'd come into my uncle's bar
After three
After work
For a shot and a beer
Guys with dirty jobs
Plumbers, fitters, lathers
Mostly Poles and Irishmen
(Jews, Italians
Went straight home
To brisket
Or managort)
Sawdust on the floor
Nice stale beer smell
Warm wood bar
Brass rail
Long, long mirror
(A hundred bottles there!)
Look into it
You'd see yourself
And guys on red stools
Either side

I loved that quiet place
Hung there after school
Played skee ball, shuffleboard

It's long gone now

I've been looking for it
(And that feeling)
Ever since

SALINAS VALLEY

Oh Salinas Valley fair,
I dream of you
Sans lettuce,
Sans spinach,
Sans broccoli,
North to south
And south to north,
Radiantly, soothingly GREEN,
But also throbbingly YELLOW,
When the sun is strongest
And the sky is bluest.
And, when the front rolls through,
All black and gray and silvery white,
On Santa Lucia crest
And Gabilan slope,
Wild, wild,
Raging wallcloud
WILD!

SANDHILL FIELD

I've read
There are a million spiders
In an acre's grass.

I didn't do the count.
(Who could?)

An anthill has, perhaps,
A thousand little ants per six-inch world.

Again, no count,
But looks 'bout right to me.

This cornfield has
Two thousand cranes per acre.

Just a guess.
I can't count—
I can barely breathe for awe.

The ravens flit around above,
Trying to cadge a few bites,
But its hopeless.
There's no room for them
In this riot of
leaping, milling, five-foot birds.

The sound?
I heard it,
But I can't remember it.
That strangeness called nothing
From memory.

If ever I come across that sight again,
I'll try to see it plain,
Save a picture of it

And its sound in my brain.

But,
I'll bet,
I won't be able to.

It's like a soundless dream.

You see it,
And you don't.

SCHUBERT, QUINTET, D956

Little man,
Young man,
Dying man
Writes this last great thing in C,
His epitaph.

Asks to hear Beethoven
One last time:
Quartet 14.

They bury him
While playing his request.

Since then,
Many have asked
To be buried
To his quintet.

I just like listening to it
In the dark.

But when the time comes,
Please play it for me

SEASONS

Even here in Cal,
I find
the subtle change
of day to day

Not in the sky,
which changes hour to hour,
but
in the market fruits and stalks and leaves,
which slowly,
slowly
change from week to week

Southwest's winter secret,
revealed to those who stay,
is bare and cold

But here,
oranges
and greens,
grown in winter,
piled on market tables,
yield

slowly

to things
red and gold
in spring

SIRENS

How do I explain to the insulated
that when I hear the siren wail,
I know it wails for me.

Oh, they say they know Donne's tolling,
but do they really, really know
it tolls for them?
I doubt it,
for if they did,
they'd throw down the book and run.

Just like my peers,
I left home early.
Set sail in my little boat,
my spirits high.
But soon the seas got rough,
and I foundered on a desert isle.

Rescued by the good witch,
I lived and became strange.
My Gulliver was happy
with the big and the small,
the crooked and the straight,
and they became my norm.

Now that I've left that place,
I fit in well enough,
but the secret's mine to tell:

This life of ease and wealth and health
Is only real to those who live it.

Another real
sleeps under the bridge,
curled up in the back of the bus,
in the tunnel,

116

and dumpster dives.

Its whiff of death and decay is faint
but there for those who stop to smell it.

It wails for thee.

SO FRAGILE

I'm X.
I've Y
And A
And B
And C
And D.
Roof overhead
Food on the table
Clothes on my back
And some money in the bank.

Bliss!

But

It's all so tenuous,
So fragile.
And connected—
A few feet down
And a mile up
In the sky.

One tremor
Flame
Rogue virus
Drought
Or quake—
It all comes crashing
Down
Down.

Woe!

I tremble.

SORT OF NATURE POEM

Seeing a redwing,
Remebering a Dodge.

Pigeons and sparrows,
My Brooklyn avifauna, 1955.
But no shortage of cars
For me to watch.

That Dodge had wings.
Tricolor, too!
Black body with
Magenta and bright green trim.

In my memory over half a century,
Brought back in marsh today
By feathered look-alike.

Chirrrrrrrrrrrrrrrrrrrrrrrrr!

SPRING DREAM

She's heading down the hole.

Prostrate on ground,
I hold her hand,
Tight,
My wrist on rim,
Chin in dirt.

And think:
Why not follow her?
Into the abyss.
Just get it done.
Had a good run,
My share of joy.
Enough.

Then:

A petal.
Another.
More.
Pink.
Down the hole they go.

It's Spring!

So I let go.
Get up.
Look at the bees.

She doesn't fall.

SPRING HAS SPRUNG

It's Spring.
Stiff wind blowing new green round.

We all bow down to Spring,
Sing songs, write poems,
Tra lala lala.
Me too,
From the time I first put spade in soil
(Fourteen?)

I think of Grandpa.
What was Spring to him?
Not much.
Just another season
In his life of toil and sickness.
Read of its arrival in his "Forvertz"
As he sipped his glessel tea upstairs.

But to Grandma,
Old-world farm girl,
Spring meant taking off her heavy coat
And waving her arms around
As she walked the Brooklyn streets
Between the vacant lots,
Looking for sorrel for her schav.

And what of my mother and father(s)?
Urban folk, always.
To them,
Spring meant rolling up the rug
(Don't ask)
And looking for the window screens.

But you!
Miss Newark to Vermont.
You put the birds and beasts to shame
With greed for green,
Which, once wakened,

121

Would not be slaked until
A hundred plants were in the ground.

In April.

They died of frost, of course.

And May snow.

Which gave you an excuse
To do it
All over again.

SUBSUMED

"They live separate lives.
I guess that's OK? Huh?"

No, not me.
I'm in all the way
Or not at all.
Passion's all that matters.
The rest is crap.

What do I mean?

If you really love,
Subsumed,
And it ends,
You'll shake:
Days,
Weeks,
Months,
Years.

But you'll feel,
In every fiber,
Intense love.

Still.

And loss.

And you'll remember all.

What do I remember?

First,
That shag.
Light brown?
Dark blonde?

Those eyes:
Gray!

That big smile.
That laugh.

And yes,
The three-inch espadrilles,
White peasant blouse,
Short shorts (!!!!)

Loving all day long
On that homemade bed.

Yes.
Feeling,
In every fiber.

Still.

That's what I mean.

The rest is crap.

SUMMATION

A life's gone by.
I sit and think of what I've done,
And feel ashamed.

I thought I'd build the Brooklyn Bridge,
The Eiffel Tower,
Cure cancer,
Write Ulysses and the Ninth.

Instead,
I made some money,
Built some houses,
Launched some books,
And had some fun.

I haven't killed, I think,
But let a lot of people down.
Perhaps I helped a few as well,
So it's a wash.

I don't expect
A call on this,
As I have no belief.

Just want to use what days I have
For good and beauty,
That I might grant me

Grace.

SUNDAY MORNING SERVICES

Sunday morning services,
Manor Lanes.

Bowling badly,
Having fun.
Talking about revolution,
Trotsky,
And the Second Front.
Old guys missing the action,
Looking for a fight.
While, outside,
Everything seems to be
Going to pot.
Poor are getting poorer.
Rich are getting richer.
And we're all getting fucked.
Blah de blah de blah-dy blah.

But . . .

In the next lane
An old black man
Is really
Knocking them down.

So, I say,
Hope you don't mind my asking—
I'm sixty-seven.
How old are you?

Seventy-nine!
Got ten years on you!

Well, says I,
Are you getting better or worse?

And I get a tale

Of sixty-something years

From
No blacks could bowl in Texas then,
But the man would let us pinboys bowl,
After closing,
As he counted his money.
And that's how I got started.

To
The Navy in Hawaii—
There was an alley on the base.

To
Here and there
Over the years,
Just for fun, you know.
Don't think much about it.
Just throw the ball.
But, you know,
You can learn a lot
From the computer.

And now I've got the gout,
And my shoulder hurts,
But I keep going.
And look,
The magic's coming back!
(He gets a four-bagger)

So I look around
At our lovely bunch
Of particolored, multilingual mugs,
Knocking them down together,
And realize that
There HAD BEEN a revolution.

I'd lived through it.
Just didn't see it.

And now I'm really feeling high,
Like I just bowled three hundred,
Times three.

Strike!

SURVIVOR DUTY

She's been burnt and boxed,
Now I must do the rest—
Box her stuff
And sell the place

Would I could just burn that, too.
But it has value
And there are neighbors

Survivor duty

I slip her key into the lock
And walk into her former life

Everything is arranged a certain way,
Has a certain scent—
Not mine

No voyeur,
I force myself to sort clothes, shoes,
Open drawers,
Sift through piles of papers, old letters,
Let the cat out

There's so much here I know
(We were close),
Yet so much I don't,
Which puzzles me

And there it is

An old letter
From someone I don't know
But from a place I do,
Which is why I don't toss it with the rest

But read instead

And find an old, awful truth,
Never shared,
But mine as much as hers

The past should stay put,
Not knock you senseless

Then I remember
The things I keep locked away.
No one will ever know them.
I'll take them with me when I go,
Unless, like her,
I get called
Before I can do the job

THALIA

FOCUS!

Sitting in the dark,
front rows near the screen,
we seem to be pitched
backward

FOCUS!!

Harpo matches Groucho perfectly
in the mirror scene.
Anna Sten beguiles silently.
Garbo sulks.
Marlene remembers some kind of man.

FOCUS!!!

Never go to the movies by yourself.

Never see a funny flick
when you're blue.

Never forget
93rd and Broadway.

FOCUS, DAMN IT!!!!

THE CALLUS

A lifetime fiddling will produce
an odd bulging muscle
near right arm's elbow

I have
Right hand
Middle finger
Left inside surface
Above the knuckle

A bump!

How many years
holding a pen
or pencil?

For a living or
just to live?

I like you,
Mr. Bump.

You define me.

THIRTY-FIVE TURKEYS

Thirty-five turkeys

Thirty-five years
Your sous-chef

Watched your arms
Chopping, stirring
But mostly
Watched your face
Joyous, intent
Making real your childhood makebelieve
Erasing years of pain
With sausage dressing
And candied yams

Thanksgiving
Your high holy day
Had to be just right
And always was with you in charge

Alone now
I sense you watching me
As I
Reach for the roasting pan

THOUSAND

The thing to remember
'bout thousand-year storms
is that they do occur

Might skip a thou or two
but happen they will

Standing in the desert talus,
looking uphill,
I see rows of rocks,
big ones,
like stone walls in Vermont,
and think,
Why bring the big Cats, Kubotas
out here to nomansland?

But looking down,
though spring and green,
I see the wash,
the waterline,
where the torrent was
and know that
when you see the thunderhead,
it's not a bad idea to run

THREADING A NEEDLE

Threading a needle,
Squinting my eye at the eye,
Remembering my Bubbie,
Doing the same for her,
When she was my age
And her eyes had failed,
As she cared for me
In her home
After school

I helped out in her kitchen
In my little-kid way,
Chopped liver, onions, and eggs
For her Yiddishe paté,
Grated potatoes
For her kugel,
And played with the dog

Then out would come
That wide-ruled notebook
With the black marbled cover,
Open to the a-b-c's,
And I would try
To teach her
The foreign tongue
That was my birthright

She was so proud of me!

But we never got to z
In her home
Above The Royal Bar and Grill,
Sutter Ave and Essex Street,
Brooklyn,
New York

Such a long,
Long
Time
Ago

TO THE CORE

Force yourself
Up and out,
Walk 'round the block,
Lest some stickiness
Break free of venous perch,
Travel brainward,
And bring the curtain down.

Then back in and down,
To work again.
As that's what you have always done?
For fear that Sloth
Will keep you bedbound
In her erotic-dream embrace?

Whence this inner rottenness?
This Puritan drive?
This need to be and do good,
Earn and churn?

Mom, Dad, Cotton Mather,
And the little busy bee?

No matter!

Take comfort in
That lovely oleander hedge.

TOOKER

Long rows of phone booths
(Already artifacts)
Changing rooms
(No doors)
Subway white-tile mazes
Barred tellers' cages
Frosted-glass cubbies
(With peepholes cut)
Wild eyes looking out

Men in raincoats
Furtive

Kerchiefed women
Anguished

Jaundiced faces
Terror in their eyes

Ochre
Raw Sienna
Warm cad red

Locked outside
Looking in

Trapped inside
Looking out

Panicked

This is the dream

The nightmare

Reality for some

138

Like him

Like me

TURNING, TURNING

How slow the gyre,
Like that new windmill
At fifteen rpm,
Blades long as a subway train.

But the pace is quickening.
It's widening, too.
Makes you nervous.

Could we slow it down?
The walls are covered with life.
You want to savor it.
It brings peace.
Any faster, it will blur.

But years go by,
And it seems,
Though there were doubts,
They may continue, so . . .

So, maybe,
Just maybe,
Hold onto your hat,
And look out the window.

UNCLOUD ME

Black dog's got me by the brain
And won't let go.
Another gray day here.
How I long to see that
Bright blue line
Above the gold.

All art's useful narcissism,
But nature doesn't care
If you live,
Or die,
Or spout,
Or draw her,
Or even think.
She lies there, perfect,
And lets you be.

Bluegold Southwest,
So rich in human ugliness,
Gives you these gifts:
Uncluttered, distilled forms,
Heat,
Clarity,
Freedom,
Peace.

UNFROZEN MEMORY

So cold today!
Wind howling.
Birds have gone someplace
To shelter.

But it's only forty-five!
I used to be that Vermont guy.
I'd have laughed at this,
Knowing minus forty.

Makes me remember.
Takes me back.

How I miss my crazy girl,
Wild,
When I was that crazy boy,
Wild,
When we were young,
Laughed at everything,
Made that little Fiat
Do three-sixties in the snow,
When that snow was just a game,
And that cold was so warm,
When Vermont was home,
And we were young.

VETERANS DAY

Veterans Day—
Cold rain falling
Car won't start
Panic
Angst
Aggro

Curse
Kick
Get a jump
Car in shop
Wait

Can't do
What I want to do

Then remember—
Veterans Day!

Think of father
Foxhole
Frozen Apennines
Penetrating wounds
To chest and limbs
KIA
December seventh
Nineteen forty-four

And feel—
Shame
Shame
Shame

WAGES OF LOSS

Sentences I end myself
Ones I hear that I no longer end
Tight lean in theater seats
Or on a plane
Or at the kitchen sink
That crazed look in the morning
Before the coffee hits
Hooded eyes at late night news
Hair tickling my nose as I
Read over your shoulder
That voice on the phone
Errands
Laughter
Nicknames
Breath

WAITING FOR THE BIG A

Grandma lost it
Age seventy.
Dumped on the parlor floor.
Saw it lying there one day.
They put her in a "home."
It stank of shit
And frightened me.
Tied her to the bed.
(Did that back then.)

"The bottoms of my pots
Are cleaner than
The insides of hers!"
She railed.
(This of a sister
Dead forty years.)

Mom was the same age
When she began to go,
But her ticker crapped out first.

Now you know why
I don't buy green bananas.

WALKING SHORE

Every day the same
And different

Owl gone from perch
Hawk
Feathered nemesis
Gone too
Crows and mallards never leave
Egret wades flat
Dry yesterday

You see
All the way
Across the bay
In fog the day before

Wigeons have arrived
Pintails still here
Stilts in pond outbound
Gone upon return

Always the same

And always new

WALKING WITH GIACOMETTI

I like to walk with Giacometti

We leave my house
Half-hour before sunset

He's behind me as we walk west
To my left as we turn south
And ahead of me as we walk east

I admire his physique
So tall!
So thin!
Long legs dark against the golden desert floor

He's silent as we walk
We stretch our arms above our heads
He's reached his apogee

Then, as we turn west again
Sun dips beneath the rooftops
And he's gone

Lured, who knows where,
By the aroma from
A dozen backyard grills

WE'RE ALL FUCKED

Expelled from bed and dream
By itchy eyes,
Burning carapace,
And cramping legs,
Drawn to mirror
By angry, itchy spot of skin
(Try not to look at ravaged face),
Look out on grayest dawn
And sketch the day's
Survival plan.

Like Marat in his tub,
Afire,
This old body's held together
By duct tape and crazy glue.

Don't eat that—
It'll get you later.
Don't sit like that—
You'll feel it when you leave the chair.
Don't have another drink—
Tomorrow you'll regret it.
Be sure to wear a hat—
Old Sol will melanoma you.

Or look around,
At empty storefronts,
Burned-out buildings,
And a land so scarred,
It's hard to see its lovely past.

And so,
The old nightmare proves true:
Caught in the deserted streets,
In your underwear,
You struggle up that steep, steep hill

As if paralyzed.

You may wake up,
But you're still
Fucked,
As are we all.

WHAT WAS ONCE

Wildflower book in hand,
I head uphill
Meadow green
To see what I can see

I see some cows
And piles of flop
And lots of grass
But then
Some close ground color:
The first one!

Shuffle shuffle
Turn turn
(Good thing there's
A color key)
Find that little orange bugger
And there I read:
NOT NATIVE

Drat!

On to the next:
Same thing!

On on on
Same thing!

Usurpers all!

Should be no surprise.
We've fouled our nest.
Why spare this place?

I long for Heidi's meadow,
Some pristine place

To run
Lie down
And see and feel
What was once

WHAT'S LEFT

Tramped clear across the continent

Only the coasts survived—
Since they could not farm the sea
(Back then)

Pillaged the rest:

Broke it
Plowed it
Mined it
Burned it
Wrecked it

So that only in the "parks"—
Those bits we wrested back
At great expense—
Can one imagine
What was once

So beautiful

It took songs
And poems
And paint
To capture
Just an intimation

Of what was
Once

So beautiful

WINTER SPRING

Crabapple thinks it's spring,
All pink on branches bare.
Magnolia, too,
Ablaze this wintry day.
Confused, but happy,
In this migrant's place.

I'm new here, too.
Don't know what next I'll see,
But happy to be shocked
By flowers on this wintry day.

The immigrant who came here once,
Brought leafy tokens of his home
To root in foreign soil
And thereby make it his.
And when he died
The plants,
Left to their own devices,
And knowing only what they knew,
Kept to their old routine,
And bloomed when they saw fit.

But I,
A stranger,
In this migrant's place,
Only care to know the new,
And smile at what I find
In springlike winter.

YOU'LL KNOW

Not Daniel Boone
Not an Injun
We have everything we need
Too much!

Want to know
What it's really like?

Take a hike
Stay overnight
Winter on
Mt. Washington

If you live
(Note: If you live)
You'll know

And when they rescue you
And patch you up
And send you home

Even if you still
Have all ten
You won't rush
To flip that switch
That silly switch
Turn on that screen
And read that crap

You'll know

ZODIACAL LIGHT

Peering through the eyepiece
in that cold place,
lit only by star and zodiacal light,
I see a galaxy
ninety-eight million light-years away

Is it still there?
If not,
What am I looking at?

The cold penetrates my gloves
Makes me shiver
But I am happy
Knowing that
One day
My dust will join yours

Our dust will blow away
And light up the sky
Someplace far away

ABOUT THE AUTHOR

Paul Schwartz,
born in
Brooklyn,
1944,
has lived in
many places
(now California)
and done lots of stuff.